Funny Clowns

by Anastasia Suen
illustrated by John Manders

Scott Foresman

Editorial Offices: Glenview, Illinois • New York, New York
Sales Offices: Reading, Massachusetts • Duluth, Georgia
Glenview, Illinois • Carrollton, Texas • Menlo Park, California

Do you like clowns?
They make work look like fun.
How do they do that?
Come along and see!

Clowns paint their faces.
They put on silly wigs.
They look in their trunks.
What do they find?
Lots and lots of funny things!

Clowns act silly for the crowd.
They make the crowd laugh.
The workmen pull things around.
The crowd doesn't watch them.
They watch the clowns.
The clowns are so funny!

Clowns like to play tricks.
This clown has a little can.
He pulls on the top.
Out pop some fake snakes!

Look at this clown with a crown.
Don't try this at home.
It's not a good idea!
This is no way to ride a bike!

What are the clowns doing now?
There is a fire!
"Jump," yell the firemen.
"Here she comes," they cry.
"There she goes!" they yell.

This clown can't find the rabbit.
He looks under his brown cape.
He turns the hat upside down.
Where is the rabbit?
It is eating a carrot!

These two clowns have a race.
It looks as if one ran out of gas!
The other one wins the race.

This clown likes to go fishing.
He puts his line down in the water.
Soon he feels a tug.
He pulls out a shark!
He'd better run for his life!

Look at these clowns.
They all ride together.
Ten clowns in one little car!
Now that's a crowd!

All the clowns take a bow.
It is time to go.
They had a great time.
They hope you did too.

Phonics for Families: This book provides practice reading words with the vowel sound heard in *clown* and spelled with the letters *ow*; words with two syllables; and the high-frequency words *pull, goes, great, idea,* and *along*. Read the book together. Then have your child name words that rhyme with *clown*.

Phonics Skill: Vowel diphthong *ow/ou/*; Medial consonants (two-syllable words)

High-Frequency Words: *pull, goes, great, idea, along*